# Purpose Money

*Achieving Purpose in Life*
*Through Focused Spending*

## SHAWN SAUNDERS

ISBN: 0692953469
ISBN 13: 9780692953464
Library of Congress Control Number: 2018901668
Shawn Saunders, Locust Grove, GA

*I dedicate this book to Kristen and Christina. You have made my every day life rewarding as your mother. You have shaped my purpose in life more than I can ever express. I love you both deeply.*

*To my mother, Mabel Minnis-Saunders. On your shoulders, I stood, knowing that you would not let me fall. You have been an amazing model of strength, resilience, and discipline. You may be gone but will never be forgotten.*

*To all those people who gave me the gift of access to their lives for the purpose of coaching them to a better understanding of self, purpose, and money. Every day you make my dreams come true. Thank you!*

# ACKNOWLEDGMENTS

To all the people who encouraged and pushed me to pursue my passion of coaching others into a better understanding of living a truly prosperous life.

The first person to recognize my gift was Hugh Thomas, Pastor of Abundant Living Ministries in Pembroke Pines, Florida. Thank you for teaching and coaching me.

I will always be grateful to Henry and Carol Fernandez of the Faith Center in Sunrise, Florida, for giving me a platform to exercise my gift.

There are no words to express adequate gratitude to Earnest Cobbs and Colamae Collymore, both of whom wholeheartedly embrace my passion. Thanks for seeing me through the eyes of my Creator and releasing me to pursue my purpose.

The friendship and wisdom of Dr. Mike Murdock over the years has proven to be invaluable. Dr. Murdock, you will always be super-special to me!

# INTRODUCTION

One of the main goals of most people is to increase their finances. Some want to get out of debt or start saving for retirement. Others want to have funds for college, investments, vacations, a home, a car, or some other major expense. Amazingly, a lot of people just want to make it through another day, week, month, or year without losing everything they have worked so hard for. Yes, there are many people who are barely getting by. They are on the verge of losing their homes, cars, and so on. Just one disruption in their income and their fragile financial world could crumble.

When living in a cycle of work, debt, and work, dreams are placed on hold. People are seeking purpose in life, not realizing that lack of finances has hindered their ability to pursue the goals that would really make them happy and bring about true prosperity.

What has this done to the emotional and psychological state of these people? They begin to live with high levels of anxiety and fear. They experience despair and feel helpless to turn around what seems to be a devastating situation. Most seem to think that if they could just make some more money or if a friend or family member helped them out, it would make life so much easier for them. All they really want is a break - another chance to get this financial situation right. And if someone would just believe in them and make a substantial investment, they could get their lives back on track.

There is one problem with this mind-set. When most of these individuals receive the help they think they need, over time they find themselves right back in the same situation again. They repeatedly need bailouts, to the emotional and financial distress of the people who enable them. In a twisted and unfair process, they sometimes become upset with people who refuse to help them - especially if those people are known to be financially stable. Their frustrations are usually associated with questions like, "Why can't they help me? They have the money," or "That person is so tight with money. Don't they know you can't take it to the grave with you?" The best one I've heard to date is, "You don't believe in me, because if you do, why won't you invest in me?"

The answer to these questions is simple. *You* are the only person responsible for making your life happen. You are the only person responsible for your daily lifestyle, dreams, visions, aspirations, or however you want to phrase it. You are the one walking around feeling unfilled because you haven't accomplished your goals or identified your purpose. It is not the responsibility of the people around you. Placing that burden on them is unnatural and unfair, because these people have dreams and goals they are trying to accomplish as well. In some cases, the people from whom you are seeking help are aware of your financial situation, your attitude toward money, and why you're in the mess you're in. They already know that helping you, even one time, will open a door that they're not prepared to deal with.

*Purpose Money* is intended to help you find the answer that lies in taking responsibility for the decisions you make that continually place you in a position of financial stress. *Purpose Money* outlines that financial success is only part of prosperity and that true prosperity means finding and fulfilling your purpose, which money will allow you to do. *Purpose Money* is intended to teach people how to be prosperous in all areas of their life, with an emphasis on money. This is a process that requires in-depth introspection, evaluation of belief systems, and progressive, deliberate steps to change your financial future. Through the application of the Moving in 3-D (desire, determination, and discipline), principle, we can all live a rewarding life through purposeful spending.

# 1

# HELP, I'M NOT WHERE I SHOULD BE!

How often has the thought of life passing you by occurred over the past month? Did you notice that every time that feeling or thought came up, you got a sense of dismay? Some of you may get a sense of urgency, believing that you need to do something right away. But what is that something that you need to do? Where do you find this something? Who can assist you? And how can you find this assistance? These are all very relevant questions, but they often go unanswered. As a result, the present need for mobilization diminishes until next time. Then, next time comes, and the cycle is repeated.

Individuals who struggle financially experience this cycle continuously. Every time there isn't enough money to pay the bills, these questions, along with the desperate need to find assistance, start circulating again. It's like the hamster walking on his wheel to nowhere.

The journey to where you should be financially begins with a clear understanding that each person must take responsibility for his or her own financial decisions. That is easier said than done until we look at what people believe and how they make the financial decisions that lead them to ruin.

*You are living today with the decisions you made yesterday. So make sure the decisions you make today are the ones you want to live with tomorrow.*

The reality is that each of us made decisions in our past that we now have to face the consequences of in our current lives. Some of us made sound foundational building choices, and as a result, we are reaping the benefits of well-placed investments that allow us to enjoy life with minimal stress. On the other hand, others made decisions regarding their finances and future as if a steady flow of cash were promised to them for the rest of their lives. They spent money without restraint, only to wake up one day and find that it is all gone. Life has passed, and their earning capacity has drastically reduced. Fear and panic set in. Suddenly, these people are trying to make lifestyle adjustments to compensate for their lack of planning for a stable financial future. This sometimes includes finding someone whose financial resources can fill the gap and possibly maintain them in the lifestyle they have become accustomed to. Now, they are deciding to make their financial future the responsibility of someone else. Again, they are not taking responsibility for the decisions they made that got them into the mess in the first place. They now want to build relationships around other people's finances with an expectation that they will ride on the tails of those people's success.

In order to change your financial future, you must examine your belief system. What are your thoughts and beliefs regarding money? How do you relate to money? What do money and its possession mean to you? Answers to these questions (and more) clarify why people make the decisions they do with their money. They provide insight into why some people have money and a secure financial future and others don't. They can explain why some people can experience financial ruin and still rebound only to be stronger financially, while others are captured in a daily downward spiral. These people are unable to focus or grow financially. They blame others for their lives and operate with an expectancy that others must help them.

To get to the bottom of these behavioral and psychological components that shape our relationship with money, we must first look at what people know and believe. I have heard it said that knowledge is power. But I have not found that to be 100 percent true. What I discovered is that only the knowledge that is believed and applied can produce power. In other words, you can read this book and find it filled with new information. At the end of this book, you will have knowledge. Your power with all this knowledge will be determined by whether or not you believe the information you learned and apply it to your life.

With all this in mind, let us look at some of the views people have of prosperity and poverty.

## Prosperity

When you ask people what prosperity is, they often reply that it means to have wealth, opulence, or riches, which is usually measured in material things and the size of one's bank account. Prosperity is viewed as being successful, flourishing, thriving, or having affluence. Most people see prosperity as synonymous with large amounts of money; expensive homes, cars, and clothes; the ability to eat and drink the absolute best at all times; vacations around the world in luxurious hotels; and traveling first class, among other things. To sum it up, it's the ability to live the way you want and do whatever your heart desires because of the size of your bank account, inheritance, and investment portfolio. Money is not a problem. The world views this form of prosperity as power. Those who have the money have the power, and the rest are delegated to serve.

Reality TV has a major impact on how people view a life of opulence, through its barrage of excessive spending and heightened sense of entitlement. Movies and other forms of media have portrayed the rich as people who got their wealth stepping on the backs and heads of others while robbing the poor to increase their fortune. So if you have it, great! And if you don't, there's a tendency to feel disenfranchised.

The problem is, looking at it from these limited perspectives can promote a twisted view of what true prosperity really is. It's one of the reasons the church has been guilty for generations of teaching a religion that has frightened its people away from financial abundance. The lack of understanding of true prosperity has caused many people to settle for a life of substandard living in the name of God who created the very nature of prosperity and provided the resources to make it happen.

The belief that we all exist on this earth for a reason, that we are all born with a purpose that culminates in a global intent of the very existence of humanity on this earth, means that prosperity has to be more than just money and its equivalents. With this in mind, prosperity can be defined as having what you need to complete your life's purpose and being able to enjoy it.

*Prosperity then becomes having the necessary resources for the path you choose for your life. Prosperity is having the financial help as you move from dreams to accomplishments. Prosperity is the ability to enjoy the journey.*

Understanding that we are all born with a purpose, our happiness comes when we identify and pursue it. Having the necessary financial and other forms of resources to complete our purpose makes life enjoyable and fulfilling. That's true prosperity. It's not the accumulation of things but the accomplishment of our goals that increases our true value. In essence, true prosperity is balance in all areas of your life: emotional, spiritual, physical, and financial.

## Poverty

Government and society use markers to determine what poverty is. If your income falls within a certain bracket or below the preset poverty line, you are considered poor. Synonyms for poverty include indigence, want, poorness, meanness, destitution, and great need (*Webster's*). Race, religion, ethnicity, and communities are also markers by which poverty is determined. These markers determine how you are categorized when it comes to funding for programs, resources of the government, and various charities. Lifestyles and decisions are built around these markers. But poverty is so much more than that.

The *Concise Oxford Dictionary* (7th ed., 1982) defines poverty as "renunciation of right to individual ownership of property; scarcity, deficiency, inferiority...situation in which increase in pay leads to no greater total income, because of the loss of benefits." Reading this definition sparked a desire in me to know more about poverty. What do I believe, and how is that affecting my current level of achievement and financial status? If poverty is a renunciation of my right to individual ownership of property, what have I disregarded in my life that could have prospered me or increased my value? How am I losing the benefits of my income despite earning more and more each year? What am I doing daily that creates or maintains this state of poverty, not only for myself but others as well?

Growing up on the island of Andros in the Bahamas, I understood that we were not rich, but I didn't realize we were poor. I had food every day. I wore clean clothes and usually had shoes or sneakers to wear daily. Being the youngest of five children, I was my mother's number-one assistant. We went to the farm together to plant and harvest food for the house. We fished, caught crabs in season, and took those to market. All this toil allowed for what I considered a well-provided life. I came to believe that heavy manual labor is required to feed your family and keep a roof over your head. So I became comfortable with that. This was a way of life that seemed normal. Everyone around me was doing the same thing. From time to time, we borrowed some rice or sugar, but for the most part, each family took care of itself. There was no government assistance available to us.

The lightbulb went on in my head that we were poor when I moved to Nassau to complete high school. Suddenly, I realized that my life was far below the standard of a lot of people living in Nassau. It was during high school in Nassau that I became aware of something called college and the various degrees. I saw people wearing fantastic clothes and shoes, driving expensive cars, living in beautiful homes with bathrooms inside the house, and shopping in grocery stores with an endless supply of stuff. I learned quickly that if I wanted to live above the standard I was raised in, I had to do something different. Keep in mind that I didn't realize how poor I was until I moved to Nassau. The whole experience of living in Nassau raised my awareness that my life was different, but it also made me realize I could change it.

After I'd been in Nassau for a while, my host family asked me to leave. I went to live with another family in a drug-infested neighborhood. Often, I was locked out of the house and had to sleep on the porch until they opened the door in the morning. After sleeping in my only uniform, I would freshen up and head right back to school, walking for miles. Every day I had the option of calling my mother so I could return home. But when I compared where I came from to where I could go, I decided that sleeping outside was a small price to pay.

I went on to finish high school and college. I went into business for myself and built a multimillion-dollar company, thinking that all these things were the keys to living a successful and prosperous life. I soon discovered that not only was prosperity more than that, but poverty was far more than I could have imagined.

I discovered I could have money, a beautiful house, a car, clothes, and so on and still be poor - poor in mind, body, and spirit.

Here's what I discovered. *Poverty is not just a socioeconomic status; it's deprivation in any area of your life.* Anywhere in your life where there is a void is a form of poverty. Lack of finances only means you don't have the necessary money to achieve the goals you've set. But what about the people who have achieved financial success? They have everything they desire that money can buy. But some of them don't have stable interactive relationships with people. They don't have successful dynamics with family or friends. At the end of the day, when the staff leaves, they are all alone surrounded by stuff that cannot provide emotional comfort. This is emotional or psychological poverty.

There are those who have family, friends, great relationships with people, and enough money, but physically their bodies are falling apart from sickness and disease. All the money in the world can't restore their health. Some would give anything just to be healthy again so they could enjoy life. This is physical poverty.

The last but most prolific type of poverty I want to talk about is spiritual poverty. Operating on the foundation that humans are part physical and part spiritual, we need to believe in something or someone. We make our decisions based on what we believe and feel. Most of our decisions are based on our belief system. People who never got the opportunity or took the time to understand who they are or who decided to pattern themselves after a belief system that does not tie into their true identity are people who wake up one day and realize that they have been living for others rather than themselves. This is spiritual poverty. It's at the core of the emotions of a person who feels their life lacks purpose. To fill this void, most people pursue religion and other forms of spirit, mind, and body exercises. The person with money can pursue mentors, coaches, and spiritual advisors to assist them in filling this void. Just imagine combining spiritual and financial poverty in the life of a person. What you end up with is a person who loses joy for life. And, if they are not careful, feelings of despair can set in.

To say that poverty is just socioeconomic is very limiting. It doesn't explain the needs and longings of people beyond the money. It doesn't explain why the only cure for money is more of it. Until there's balance in the psychological, physical, and spiritual being, money will never be seen for what it really is: a tool.

# 2

# POVERTY MIND-SET

Remember that story I told you about how I didn't realize how poor I was until I moved to Nassau? That story is vitally important to the way my life turned out. You see, all that I learned from my mother - getting up early, working hard, and then getting excited over the below-minimum income she brought in - became the core of the lifestyle and mind-set I developed. Being around people who appeared to have it all together and seeing the grandeur of their lives stirred up a passion for success in me. On Sunday afternoons, I would ride with my friends into the affluent neighborhoods of Nassau to look at the big, beautiful homes and dream of my "one day."

Guess what? That "one day" came. As a professional, I began to make really good money. My initial instinct was to purchase everything I had desired but was denied because of money. I bought tons of clothes, shoes, things I needed, and things I didn't know if I needed. I just wanted it because I could afford it. I gave money and gifts to family, friends, and people I didn't know. Anyone with a sad story could get money out of me. People came out of the woodwork, and I took care of them all.

Those Sunday afternoon drives paid off as well. Because I fell in love with beautiful properties, I also bought quite a bit of real estate. I comforted myself by saying that I had investment properties that eventually would pay off. In my mind, I just needed to own the property regardless of whether it generated income.

My mind-set toward money is what governed my earning, spending, saving, and investing. This became apparent to me when I began to slowly unravel as my health declined. Having a doctor tell me that I could die at the age of forty-six if I didn't make some drastic life changes hit me like a ton of bricks. Two weeks in bed gave me nothing to think about other than that I really hadn't lived or enjoyed my life. Suddenly, I could think of all the things I wished I had done with my life. I thought of all the people I wished I had taken the time to love. The places I should have visited. The cultures I wanted to experience. But the most important realization was that all the material possessions didn't matter like I thought they did. As I laid in bed in my home, surrounded by paid help, I wondered where all the people I had been so generous to were. Surely after a few days, weeks, or months they would call if they didn't hear from me. And guess what? They did call, but it was not until they missed the crutch of my financial support. They called not because they hadn't heard from me and were concerned. They called because I wasn't doing what I normally did for them, which was to pay for their lives and dreams.

That experience triggered a soul search that led to a change in mind-set and behaviors toward my life and money. It caused me to explore who I am and for what reason I am here on this earth. In this journey of discovery, I realized many things. The most profound was that even though I had achieved success in my life, I was still operating with a poverty mind-set that proved to be destructive to my friends, family, and relationships.

*The poverty mind-set is a subconscious belief system that governs our destructive, conscious decisions regarding money, its possession, and spending.*

The poverty mind-set is a form of mental slavery that drives people to want more, but only for momentary gain and pleasure. It enforces the behavior of wanting more just to have more, to be noticed or accepted by society and within certain social groups under the illusion that this open display of materialistic possessions is true success and prosperity. This mind-set has not only left many financially devastated but caused some to lose family, friends, and relationships that could never be repaired.

Introspection revealed that my attitude toward money is what caused me to do the things I did. Watching my mother work hard instilled the mind-set that I must always work hard for everything I wanted. But I didn't equate that to others working for their own stuff. I gave it to them. I looked at people in their situations, and empathy and pity took over. I used my finances to resolve their issues. My mind-set was that I didn't want people to experience unnecessary pain or hardship, especially if it was within my power to help them. What I now know is that pain is a motivator. When people are fearful or get tired of pain, they become motivated to eliminate it. Let them experience pain long enough, and they will seek a solution.

Another mind-set that I struggled with was having made it out of poverty when I knew so many people who were still struggling.

This included family, friends, and associates. I spent money trying to bring their lifestyle up to the level of mine. I gave gifts and vacations so they could experience a degree of opulence. Most times I carried people along to places and experiences because I didn't want to have the experience by myself. So instead of rewarding people for their loyalty or faithfulness in our relationship, I just didn't want to be alone. My self-esteem was a mess. I felt some degree of guilt over having more than the people I had known most of my life. This also caused me to minimize my achievements when speaking to people. And I was unable to accept compliments from others.

The point I'm making here is that your thoughts and actions regarding money started during your childhood. The people with whom you experienced life have shaped the way you earn, spend, and save money. If those people had little money-management experience, they couldn't teach you much. As we grow, we either recognize the need for change or embrace our behaviors as normal. Like me, some people don't know that there is a mind-set, a subconscious behavior that is governing their relationship with money and the other areas of their lives. So, they live every day believing they have their situations under control.

Looking at society today, there are many professionals who earn millions of dollars and yet retire in financial distress. They can't account for the money they've earned other than to say they had a great time while it lasted and they helped countless people. In financial ruin, they wish they had helped themselves. In the moment, they thought they were doing the right thing. Their motives were great, but they left one person out of the equation, and that was themselves. Hindsight becomes the best sight.

There's a way to change behaviors before they become destructive. It all begins with recognizing that you may have an issue. You may need to shift your thinking and behavior.

Here is an abbreviated list of questions to ask yourself:

1. Do you collect or hoard clothes, shoes, pocketbooks, or household items, including food?
2. Do you collect or hoard friends? Do you tend to want your friends to be committed to only you; not wanting to share friends with others?
3. Do you always need to have the latest and greatest of whatever excites you (cars, electronics, gadgets, trinkets, etc.)?
4. Do you always need to have excess around you to feel secure (food, toiletries, household cleaning products, etc.)?
5. Do you only want to give away what you don't value?
6. Are you mean and stingy toward others despite the enormity of your resources?
7. Are you not satisfied with just one of certain things (e.g., do you buy multiple of the same shoes, jackets, and so on, but in different colors)?
8. Do you need to have what others have, and must it be bigger and better?
9. Do you need to be the center of attention through the outward flashing of your possessions?
10. Do you need to be the center of attention, always talking about yourself and bragging about your accomplishments?
11. Do you have a sense of unworthiness despite how much you have accomplished?

12. Do you feel a sense of guilt over having become successful while family, friends, and other relations didn't?

13. Are you comfortable buying expensive gifts for people but not for yourself?

14. Do you feel the need to drag past alliances and family along with you despite their lack of discipline for accomplishment?

15. Do you feel the need to downplay your accomplishments to make others feel better despite its negative impact on you?

16. Do you feel the need to give away your finances just to maintain a relationship with a person?

There are many other questions or scenarios, but the goal here is to awaken the possibility that this could be you. If you answered yes to at least one of these questions, it's time for self-evaluation through introspection. You could be living your life with a poverty mind-set despite being a successful person. If you answered yes to three or more of these questions, you could be living with a poverty mind-set despite the amount of your success and financial resources. Recognizing the mind-set allows you to explore ways in which to change it.

How does the poverty mind-set cause a person to end up or stay poor? Let's look at the definition of poverty from the *Concise Oxford Dictionary* again. It says poverty is the *"renunciation of right to individual ownership of property*; scarcity, deficiency, inferiority...situation in which *increase in pay leads to no greater total income, because of the loss of benefits."*

Let's investigate "renunciation of right to individual ownership of property." This plays out in the lives of so many people daily without them even being aware of what they are doing. Here are some examples:

1. The exchange of your goods or services for currency is how you earn a living. Once you have completed the services or delivered the goods, you have now earned the right to compensation. It's your property. You renounce or give up your right to this money by the following:

   a. Using credit cards. Excessive use of credit takes away your right to current and future earnings. Every time you obtain the right to a paycheck, you have to give it to the creditor.

   b. Making promises and commitments to the lifestyle or dreams of others without verification or guarantee of a return on your investment. You give people your money without securing a way to get it back.

2. You may relinquish your dreams and vision for the future, settling for the easy road to avoid hardship, conflict, or effort. You know that what's inside you is the key to your prosperity, yet you give up the right to see it come to pass because of fear of the unknown. It's too hard. It puts you at odds with people who don't believe in you, so you give up and settle for mediocrity.

3. You may give away real estate, investment portfolios, cars, art, and so on in the event of a divorce or death in the family. In the arguments of a settlement, things are said and done that cause tremendous offense and pain. For some, the goal is to walk away with as much as they can, while others just want what they call "peace." In this stressful

exchange, you give others whatever they want just so they will shut up and go away. You say you just don't want trouble, but the reality is that you increase their value in the process of giving up your rights to what really belonged to you. It's a false sense of humility to cover for your lack of willingness to fight for your property.

Let's examine "increase in pay leads to no greater total income, because of the loss of benefits."

**Scenario**: You have worked on this job for two years without a pay increase. You have consistently earned $500 per week for the past two years. One day your boss raises your pay to $600 per week. You're excited. Now you can finally get a savings plan together. Weeks and months go by, and there's still no savings plan. In fact, you are still struggling to make ends meet just as you did when your salary was $500 per week. What happened? Where did the money go? You're earning an extra $100 per week but have nothing to show for it. The increase of $100 does not give you any benefit. You experienced an increase in pay but no increase in benefits.

We believe sometimes that if we got an increase in salary or if a person would loan or give us more money, it would improve our lives. The problem is, if you don't deal with the underlying issue as to how you spend and handle money, it will be of no benefit to you. You will be right back asking people for financial support over and over again. This happens through

1. unfocused, unnecessary spending;
2. impulsive spending through the need for immediate gratification; and
3. overindulgence in cravings wrapped as need.

Over time, these along with other behaviors can cause anyone to lose not only financially but also physically, psychologically, and spiritually.

### Religion and the Poverty Mind-Set

I could not complete this book or even the conversation on poverty and the poverty mind-set without addressing the issue of religion and its effect on how a lot of people view and deal with money.

Religion plays a part in the lives of millions of people in this world. It's the means by which many people make decisions about their lives, money, mates, and so on. So it's not surprising that religion also plays a part in how a person views prosperity and the accumulation of wealth. For Christians, wealth or financial abundance is considered something to be less desired because of its potential negative impact on their spiritual wealth. The tendency is choose one or the other, but a person couldn't have both.

There was a period when I questioned the value of religion in my life and its benefit. I grew up as a "Christian" believing that Jesus Christ is the Messiah and the only way to receive eternal life. I was taught that it was better to be humble in the eyes of people and God, that this is where the true blessings as a Christian lie. I went to church services every Sunday and attended Bible study through the week, developing a deep love for my religion and Jesus Christ.

As the years went by, I couldn't help but notice that all my dedication to the religion and embrace of the person of Jesus didn't really change the quality of my financial life. Yes, I had learned to love people, turn the other cheek when offense occurred, and offer a lending hand to a person in need. But I was still struggling with the idea of prosperity and living a life of abundance rather than lack. I was a professional, working and making good money but still operating within the confines of poverty by living paycheck to paycheck. All my extra finances went to the church and other religious organizations. Then one day I heard someone speaking on the fact that God wants us blessed, healthy, and prosperous. I understood the blessed and healthy part, but what did it mean to be prosperous?

In 1999, with hesitance, I began reading "The 9 Steps To Financial Freedom" by Suze Orman and quietly implemented the steps in the book. I understood that within the confines of the religion of the church, it was like a taboo to speak of wanting financial abundance. To even say that you wanted to be a millionaire was almost like swearing against the name of Jesus. Yet inside me I recognized that in order to carry out the long list of life-changing mission work I wanted to do, the finances needed to come from somewhere. I began to realize to successfully fulfill any of the church's goals required finances and a lot of it. It was the reason I was always giving my financial resources to the church.

In my book *The Covenant of Peace*, I wrote that Christians are among the poorest of all religious people. In a study conducted in 2003, it was found that Jews were the wealthiest of all religious people. Despite the fact that there are more scriptures in the Bible that deal with prosperity than salvation, the church continues to emphasize salvation more than it encourages Christians to prosper. The same applies to health and healing. More emphasis is placed on healing than prevention and healthy living. Christianity has either ignored its importance or taught that wealth and abundance are terrible things.

Christianity recognizes there are two types of wealth: financial and spiritual. Christians have a tendency to minimize the importance of money while greater emphasis is placed on spiritual wealth. As a result, a lot of Christians have achieved spiritual accolades while they live daily in desperate need of financial assistance. As religious organizations prosper through the sacrificial charitable contributions of its members, their followers struggle to grasp an understanding of how to live in a world based on economics.

As you watch the media, there are numerous articles and programs promoting negativity regarding wealth. These negative projections have been embraced by the church as justification for many to avoid wealth. Over time a fear of financial prosperity has been fostered in the church with the quoting of scriptures like "It's easier for a camel to go through the eye of a needle than for a rich man to enter the Kingdom of God" and "Blessed are the meek." But meekness has nothing to do with "brokeness." Because the ultimate goal of every Christian is to qualify for entry into the Kingdom of God when they die, why make it harder by amassing great wealth? The mind-set that "I just want to make it while I'm here on earth until I can enter the pearly gates of heaven and see Jesus" has left many operating at levels far below their full potential. They have settled into a false sense of humility, not realizing that if you are not God's hands extended in the earth, you have failed as a Christian who believes in Jesus Christ. The commission of all Christians is to help the poor, widowed, and fatherless and ensure justice for the oppressed. How do you accomplish this without money? How do you impact the world with barely enough to pay your own bills?

A balance between spiritual and financial prosperity should be of importance to the Christian. Securing a spiritual perspective is great, but being able to demonstrate what you believe through the lives impacted by your financial strength resonates with and is remembered by people. It gives the Christian a greater sense of purpose with the ability to see the results of financial investment.

# 3

# INTENT VERSUS PURPOSE

One of the questions I get from a lot of people is, "How do I identify my purpose in life? How do I discover the reason for which I was born?" It's a very deep and exploratory question that I am not sure I know the correct answer to. The questions I ask everyone are, "When you look at your life, family, society, or the world, what bothers you the most?" and "Whose life, what situation, or what circumstance would you change if you could?" The key to your purpose lies in the answers you come up with. More and more you will realize that it doesn't matter how many inspirational, motivational self-help sessions you attend. At the end of the day, your true purpose lies in your self-examination of who you are, your qualities, strengths, and weaknesses. Until you understand who you are and the true reason for your existence, your mind-set toward money and its purpose may be twisted.

*If your life is a journey with a purpose, then how will you accomplish it without help?*

How can you make it a pleasant one? If you believe that you were created and born into this world with a purpose, then you must examine the requirements of the purpose, the requirements of the environment (what nature provides and the world we live in), and the financial requirements. After all, you should never begin a project without first examining the cost and how you will be able to complete it. This should all be fully assessed before you start. This process of examination forces us to face the reality of the areas where there is a need for additional support. These areas of deficit (poverty) should now be the target of our focus for increase so we are not hindered in accomplishing our purpose. Once these areas are strengthened, we now have help for our journey. Great purpose requires great resources!

Arriving at the destination of living life with and on purpose creates a paradigm shift as to how we view money and its purpose for our lives. Focused or purpose money forces you into a position of self-examination as funds become available to you.

It sounds fantastic to say live life with purpose. I see lots of people getting excited over the fact that they have discovered their purpose in life. Some find it earlier than most, and that's fantastic!

I was a late bloomer. After building a multimillion-dollar pharmaceutical research company, I realized that there was still something missing from my life. There seemed to be a lack of determination to make more money. Even though I had achieved a certain level of success, purchased a lot of things, and was living comfortably, there still seemed to be some form of void. I soon realized that all my focus to that point had been based on "making it." Proving to people around me that I was not the poor little girl from the islands anymore. Demonstrating to those who had rejected me that I didn't need them or their social circles. I was a woman holding my own.

Having accomplished the goal I had relentlessly aspired to, I soon ran out of steam. I lost my passion for life and accomplishment. I had made it - now what? That's when I realized that my greatest passion for life came when I had a goal or a purpose for which I was striving. I needed to find another passion. I needed something that was bigger than making money to shove in the faces of people whom I barely knew and who didn't really care to know me. I needed to identify my purpose for my own sense of accomplishment regardless of what people thought of me.

### Intent

My success has all been in the discovery - discovery of new things, experiences, and so on. So, of course, the key to my success came in the discovery that in order to identify my purpose, I had to understand something called "intent." For what reason was I born, and into which situation or circumstance do I fit?

Whether you believe in evolution or creation, we wonder sometimes, "Where did I come from? Why was I born the way I am, into this family, these circumstances? Why did life happen the way it did for me? Why was I born this race or gender? Why was I born in this part of the world? Why couldn't my life be different?" We sometimes even go further by saying, "If only I…" That statement, "If only I…" is the key to identifying purpose through intent.

Identifying intent is the precursor to identifying your purpose. Your purpose is the prerequisite to understanding money. Once you identify your purpose, you will then begin the process of understanding that *money is a tool to be used for the accomplishment of your purpose.*

The creation model says that the world, the earth, the heavens, humans, animals, trees, and so on are all created by God. God, in the Bible, created our very existence over a period of six days. But what did God create all this for? Did God create just to create? Was all this part of a supernatural plan? A supernatural intent?

Let us look at intent from a business perspective. When a business plan is developed, several components are covered. We start off with an executive summary, which gives you a snapshot of what the company is about. There's also the mission statement, but more importantly, there's a vision statement. The vision sums up the reason for the formation of the company and its main goal or focus. The vision is the intent of the company. It says, "We are in business for the sole purpose of..." Anyone reading this should understand that company.

Let's use a charitable organization as our example for the discovery of intent and purpose.

The charitable organization writes its vision and mission statements. They present these to a potential contributor. Some contribute, and others walk away. The answer as to why some give and others don't is based on the individual's ability to identify with the intent (vision) of the charitable organization. How does this happen? When potential contributors see, hear, and feel the vision, they begin to visualize how they fit into the vision. They begin to identify with the vision, see themselves as part of the vision, and begin the process of self-evaluation as to how they can fit into the vision and make it happen. The contributors begin to see their *potential* for the vision. Their potential could be their skills, training, expertise, or finances. Identifying their potential then ties each contributor to the vision (intent) through the investment of their time, skills, and resources. Now this contributor has a purpose for that intent (vision). Some may offer to be employed, others volunteer, and others will finance the vision. Each serves a purpose.

Collectively, each person's potential is what qualifies that person for the purpose he or she serves for the vision.

The same principle applies to life. If God created the world with an intent (vision), then all of us are part of that vision with a role (purpose) to fulfill. If God created the world so that all creation would live harmonious, peaceful, and prosperous lives, then you will begin to understand that how, when, where, and why you were born are all part of your potential for the purpose for which you were created. It's up to you to identify your uniqueness that sets you apart from others. This uniqueness is what makes your journey special. It makes your life purposeful.

## Purpose

After understanding intent and its ability to help identify your potential, the next step is to understand purpose. Purpose is the reason or "calling" for which a person considers he or she was born. It's the motivating factor behind the decisions we make when it comes to life. It influences our choice of career, mate, lifestyle, where we live, and how we spend money.

*Purpose is having a deliberate, predetermined focus for a specific accomplishment.*

This sense of purpose is what drives your passion (desire) and determination for achievement. Without purpose, decisions are made in the moment and are sporadic. Without purpose, there is a strong likelihood that others will assign a destination for your life and money.

What does all this have to do with money? Everything! Your identification with money and the way you spend, save, or invest all comes back to what you believe and feel. Taking a moment to observe people in your environment can tell you a lot about their attitudes toward money and their underlying emotions and beliefs. One of the purposes of this book is to make you aware of the behaviors and beliefs that have shaped your financial life and how to identify ways in which to change it for the better.

This book is not just about teaching financially poor people how to live a better life. It's also about teaching people how to be prosperous in all areas of their life with an emphasis on money.

There are many people who are not poor. They have managed to raise themselves above the ranks of poverty and defied the odds that were set against them. These people, regardless of race or ethnicity, have managed to carve out a satisfactory piece of life for themselves and their family. Most are able to maintain this lifestyle for generations and have died happy, surrounded by family and friends.

On the other hand, there are those who managed to get out of poverty only to find themselves back where they started or teetering on the edge of inevitable doom. These are the ones who made the money and for numerous reasons either lost it all or spent it on stuff that was not able to build or sustain them. These people operate with the poverty mind-set. Their actions have taken them down a destructive path that denied them the ability to increase what they have been given.

It is said that necessity is the mother of all invention. That may be so because as progress continues around us, we are forced to reinvent our approach to life. Now that each person has a right to an education and minimum-wage stipulations are in effect, along with other policies, reinvention has caused a shifting of mind-set. It doesn't matter how much money you make. What became the focus is how much people can get you to spend on goods and services that you've been led to believe are necessary for life. This is having purpose assigned to your money without any input from you. You then are walking out someone else's intent, which is to take your money, thereby stripping you of your power.

Who cares if you earn a lot of money? As long as I can get you to spend it so that it benefits me and not you, who cares that you are earning hundreds of thousands or possibly millions of dollars? It takes us right back to the definition of poverty stating that *"increase in pay leads to no greater total income because of the loss of benefits."* Every time people spend their hard-earned money on meaningless stuff, they are losing the benefit of that money. It's the poverty mind-set in its most fashionable form. It's why a struggling single mother would take her limited finances and buy expensive designer sneakers for a child. It's the reason you can find storefront sneaker outlets in underprivileged neighborhoods, while upscale neighborhoods require that you go to a mall to find the same store.

When you look around society today, there are many signs of the poverty mind-set, signs of life without purpose. The movies, TV, and other forms of media provide a barrage of celebrities who have risen through the ranks, paid their dues, and achieved status and financial gain. Yet as you observe their habits, you realize that they are still wrestling with the ghosts of lives past. They overindulge in stuff that has no value other than a temporary good feeling in an attempt to impress people who don't even know them or have any significance in their lives. Overt behaviors demonstrate their subconscious belief systems that remain unchecked and undisciplined from childhood all the way through to their current state.

While I used celebrities to make my point, this remains true of so many other people. It's just that celebrities are more visible. When people do not know and understand who they are, they are unable to identify their purpose outside of others. A person without purpose is a person without focus. A person without focus is a person who will fail at whatever he or she does. Lack of focus causes a decrease in value for life. We lose sight of the reason for which we live. Increase in wealth means nothing on a psychological level, because life itself lacks purpose. We do all the things we do just to fit in and be accepted by others. We misinterpret tolerance for acceptance. Broken focus, loss of self-identity, combined with a lack of purpose diminishes the significance of money.

Purpose comes when there is a clear vision (intent) of the path one choses to take in life. Self-identity and love combined with a desire for fulfillment propels people into purposeful living. Living with purpose now means that your financial resources have a predetermined assignment. The handling of your finances is deliberate and with specific focus. It's purpose money.

# 4

# PURPOSE MONEY

Take a moment and reflect on your earliest memory of money. Think about when you first realized the significance of money. You will most likely have an image of the environment in which you were raised and the person who raised you. This is someone who more than likely taught you most of what you know about money. This sets the foundation as to how you respond to money then and now. If the person had little to no regard for money, most likely you don't either. On the other hand, if that person worked hard, saved money, and made strategic purchases and investments, you most likely follow his or her example.

A challenge in modern society, given the ease with which credit is so readily available, is to get people to strategize for their future and the things they want to accomplish. With money in hand and lots of it continuing to come into our lives, the tendency is to delay setting strategic goals for a comfortable future. When you implement a deliberate strategy with your money, you can create the future you desire, because you are spending money with purpose.

*Purpose money is money that is preassigned or designated for a specific outcome.*

Purpose money is a process by which you deliberately allocate in your mind and determine in your heart what you will spend your money on before you receive it. By preassigning the money to a predetermined goal, you have allocated not only how it will be spent but also what it will do for you.

This may sound complex, but the reality is that we do it all the time. The only problem is that a lot of people don't preassign their money to increase their net worth. They focus on immediate gratification and end up losing most of their earnings with their value depreciated.

You will hear people say things like:

"Girl, when I get my tax return, I'm going to get me those purple shoes I've been longing for."

"I just worked twelve hours overtime to put a down payment on a car."

"As soon as I save eight hundred dollars, I'm going on vacation."

These are all preassigned designations for anticipated money. Each of these situations already assigned purpose to the money. The same is true for the individual who wants to develop a diverse financial portfolio. Instead of spending money on things that depreciate over time, the person deliberately invests in ventures that have a significant potential to increase his or her financial worth. Options such as life and health insurance, real estate, fine art, stocks, and bonds are all part of the diversity with which an individual can increase his or her net worth. The disciplined individual takes the time to explore these options and make sound decisions that have the potential to increase his or her worth.

Whether you realize it or not, every day you are spending money for a particular reason. It either increases your bottom line or decreases it. At this point, I would encourage you to think about how you spent your money over the past two weeks. How much of that money is still a part of your life? How much went to the benefit of someone else? Do you even know how your last two paychecks were spent, or did it just disappear before you could even catch a breath?

Tracking your money and retaining it within your control for as long as possible is vital. Those who invest in rental income not only maintain the value of the property for themselves but also find that the financial return is continuous. Those who go a step further and own the property-management company in addition to the income property are now spending money with themselves and retaining the revenue in their lives longer. They end up with a greater financial reward than a person who is renting or even owns a home. A home may increase your net worth, but it's not a source of income. Unless you can fix everything in the house by yourself, you will constantly have expenses associated with a home without any income.

Real estate is just one of the many ways in which you can spend money to make money. Working for your money is a great investment of your time, talent, and strength. To give it away or not receive any benefit from it will cause you to feel under accomplished. The thing to keep in mind is that every time you are about to spend money, you want to ensure that there is a benefit in it for you. The benefit may be as simple as seeing the joy on the face of someone who receives a well-deserved gift from you. While making other people happy can bring about a good feeling, securing your own financial future will promote excitement and self-confidence.

On a spiritual level, I consider money to have its own *personality*. It loves who loves and respects it. It will stay with those who demonstrate an affectionate respect for it. It is attracted to other people who share a mutual affectionate respect for money, drawing them into social groups we call circles or cliques. The wealthy become friends with the wealthy, the rich with the rich, the middle class with the middle class, and the poor with the poor. Throughout society you will see such circles of people who basically hang out with others of like mind. It seems to be a natural phenomenon that a rich person just gravitates toward another. The same happens in other socioeconomic groups. I attribute this to the personality of money, which covertly draws people together.

To answer the question of how this happens, I will say that there is a message that each person sends when he or she enters the presence of another. This message determines whether or not these individuals are receptive to each other and the dynamics with which they interact. The initial assessment is based on dress, cleanliness, body language, and speech. Content of conversation gives an idea of the person's level of education and experiences. Social skills expose the person's level of maturity, world exposure, and wisdom. Dining etiquette reveals the dynamics under which they were trained or socialized. Collectively, all these demonstrate what I call the "content of character."

This content of character is what allows a person to assess whether you are someone with or without money. It subconsciously puts you in a category in the minds of the people you interact with. Each category has a set of defined behaviors that draw each other to a place of comfort due to similarities.

With this in mind, content of character is what motivates a person to spend money on superficial, non-income-producing possessions. There is a need for love and belonging. Each person wants to be accepted and possibly loved by another. Spending money to present an image is common especially for individuals who have less than the group they want to be accepted by. You will see people spending money on expensive clothing, shoes, jewelry, and cars because they want to be perceived as fitting into a certain social group. They are looking for that initial response of visual acceptance when they enter an environment. It opens the door for conversation.

Spending this time and money just for social acceptance does not increase your value. But if you are strategic and have assessed the social or business environment you need to penetrate, it may be worthwhile to make the financial investment in your appearance.

When I first started my pharmaceutical research company, I really needed physicians to sign up under my company to get this work done. It takes billions of dollars to bring a new drug to market. In order for a pharmaceutical company to get their new drug approved for market, they collaborate with research centers around the world that collectively provide the safety and efficacy data for these new drugs. My company was one of these collaborations. Seeing that I was not a physician, I needed that alliance to make my business successful. When I first started, I was driving a Toyota Corolla. The doctors would see my car and wouldn't take me seriously. How could this woman bring hundreds of thousands of dollars to their practice and still drive a Corolla? So I changed to a Volvo. This worked better. I had my clothes right, and now with the car, accessories, and pocketbook, I looked like a woman who could increase their net worth.

As I continued to grow in business, I had to change the style and pricing of my clothes along with the car to demonstrate a visual image that I knew what I was doing. I had to convince my doctors that if I could drive such an elaborate car and wear expensive clothes, I knew how to make money. This made them feel I could do it for them. With my knowledge and skills, I knew I was capable of doing my job, but the doctors didn't know that. I needed my clients to perceive my worth from a distance so they would give me the opportunity to demonstrate my skills. My presentation gave the doctors a level of confidence in my abilities. This was the beginning of dynamic business relationships. It was also money spent with the purpose of increasing my business.

I watched a documentary that highlighted a school in a European country with a focus on training women how to attract and acclimate to the life and environment of the rich. The main focus was to train these women to date and marry rich men. While the documentary didn't mention the cost, even the investment of time and energy is still a lot. When I saw the documentary, I couldn't help but think of purpose money. The money, time, and energy spent on this training were preassigned and designated to prepare these women with the necessary skills to attract and marry a rich man. I had never heard of that before but had to respect that it was a beautiful example of how disciplined spending can get you almost anything. The men they meet and possibly marry understand the role of these women. They also understand that engaging with one of them now means their money has an additional assignment, which is to maintain this highly trained woman.

While I may mention the women first, there are men who do something similar. They dress, speak, and socialize with women whom they target based on their net worth. They give the appearance of having it all together. They come across as strong, independent defenders and protectors, winning the confidence and affection of the woman. Soon after, she finds herself in the middle of a relationship in which she is expected to carry the financial responsibilities of a man who has nothing other than the image he created. While the purpose of her money was to increase her net worth, his money was purposed for attracting a woman with money so she could pay for his life.

In both scenarios, the woman and the man preassigned their money to creating the image and skills for attracting a mate with large financial resources. While it may not be palatable to some, it was still money spent with purpose. The acceptance of such life situations is based on the content of the character of the persons involved. Each person will display his or her idiosyncrasies and psychological strengths or weaknesses.

How you spend your money demonstrates a lot about the content of your character. People who spend money to be accepted in certain socioeconomic cultures can become disillusioned with life when the true characters of the other people are revealed. What they mistook for acceptance becomes evident as tolerance. They begin to realize that some people pretended to accept or even love them in an attempt to take from them. In the end, these people were only tolerating them as a means to an end.

The purchase of my first home is my initial memory of purpose money. Once I found the house I liked, I worked overtime, cut my spending to basics, and saved every penny toward the purchase. As the time for closing on the house drew near, I realized I needed more money. I calculated how much money I needed, configured it into the number of hours of overtime, then worked the extra hours to get the money. Every penny I earned was preassigned to the purchase of my home. Because of my desire and determination to own a home, I disciplined my work and spending habits to achieve my goal. It formed the basis of my "Moving in 3-D" principle that I teach during coaching sessions.

The Moving in 3-D principle states that you can achieve anything in life if you move with desire, determination, and discipline. Once you develop or discover purpose for your money, it takes desire, determination, and discipline to accomplish your goal. It becomes an ongoing process of self-evaluation and affirmation.

# 5

## NOW WE KNOW!
## NOW WE PURPOSE!

Knowledge becomes powerful when you understand how to apply it to your everyday life. Arriving at this point, we now know what true poverty and prosperity are, along with the identifying behaviors of the poverty mind-set.

We now understand that poverty is not just the absence of money but also an imbalance in your physical, psychological, and spiritual state. Some people have tremendous amounts of money but poor interpersonal relationships; some lack a fulfilling family life or have poor health. The financially strapped person may have great family relationships and friends and even be in good health, but being unable to cover the basic necessities of life can create emotional distress.

So how can we fix this? How can we turn all this around without having to work extra hours? How do we come to a place of balance in our lives? How do we create a financial future that decreases stress? For this you will need the Moving in 3-D principle.

You must desire and be determined to change because this will drive your discipline. Without discipline, you will not achieve any of the steps to follow.

## Steps to Change

1. **Be honest with yourself.** Take the time to introspect and recognize the areas of deficits within yourself. Admit the deficiency, and be willing and committed to change. If you know that you're not the best person to handle finances in the relationship, let the one who is do it. If you don't have someone to be accountable to, find someone you trust who will question you from time to time to ensure you are on the right path.

2. **Examine the reasons why you spend money the way you do.** How do you feel when you spend money? Do you feel elated, satisfied, guilty, or even depressed? Are you spending money on friends, family, or relationships because you want to make other people happy? What happens when you see their happiness? How does that make you feel? Did you spend the money on others so that they would accept you into their circle or because they make you feel responsible for helping them? Do you feel the need to put others' needs ahead of your own? Would you buy gifts (especially expensive ones) for other people but not invest the same amount or more in yourself?

3. **Determine whether you are a spender, saver, or hoarder.** Do you like spending money because it makes you feel good? Are you an emotional shopper? Do you save money regularly? Can you wait for a sale to purchase an item, or

do you always have to purchase everything right away? Do you save money but never spend any of it? Are you always consciously saving for a rainy day even if it means not buying items that you need? Are you afraid to not have money, so you just don't spend it?

4. **Examine your current level of achievement.** Have you achieved the things you would have liked to achieve at this stage of your life? If not, what are the top five reasons why you haven't made your goals? If financial support of others is in your top five reasons, how do you feel when you are around the people you have helped, especially if they have excelled beyond your level of achievement? Do you feel anger, bitterness, or resentment toward people who constantly ask for your financial support with no regard to your feelings or financial stability?

5. **Exercise the "Power of No."** Your initial step is to begin to say no to your destructive spending habits. Say no to purchasing coffee, fast food, and other nonessential items on a daily basis. Say no to all nonessential purchases of clothing, shoes, pocketbooks, cars, electronics, magazine subscriptions, club memberships, or upgraded cable or satellite television options. Say no to expensive travel, social events, and dining out. The next step under the Power of No is to tell everyone who asks you for money, "No." Whether it is to borrow or pay a bill for someone, you are to say no to every request for your money regardless of who it is. One of the keys to success over your finances is to master the art of saying no to yourself and others truthfully. This exercise increases discipline. It doesn't mean you can't help others in the future, but you must secure yourself first.

*A word of caution*: When you start telling people no, some of them will become upset or even angry with you. They may say or do things that upset you or hurt your feelings. But keep this in mind: a person's true character comes out when they are under pressure. Saying no will show you their true character faster and cheaper than living with them. People's response to your denial of what they want from you will show you not only who they really are but also what they truly think of you. Here is where you will need to be strong. All behaviors may not be what you expect, and you may lose friends and family members. A person who truly cares about you will be understanding and supportive of your efforts to improve yourself. Deal with the others as the need arises.

6. **Establish the "No Account."** Extreme discipline is required here. On a daily basis, you are to journal and attach a monetary value to each item or request you say no to. For example, if you are a person who buys coffee every morning to the tune of $5, every time you decide not to buy the coffee, write it down in your journal with the amount next to it. Later that day, a friend calls and asks you for a loan of $20. You tell the person no and then document the loan request in your journal. This is to be a daily routine. At the end of each day, add up all the expenses you said no to. In the example above, the one-day total is $25. At the end of each week, add up your daily totals for that week. If you said no to $25 per day, your weekly total will be $175. This is the money that you now will place into the No Account. What do I mean by the "No Account"? The No Account is a bank account that you open specifically for saving all the money you accumulate from saying no to yourself and

other people. If you normally get paid every two weeks, you are to take that money from your paycheck and put it into a separate bank account. For example, if you said no to $175 per week, two weeks of that will total $350. You are to deposit $350 into your No Account. After two paychecks, you will have approximately $700 without having to work an extra day or hour. The only thing required for this savings is discipline in the ability and consistency of saying no!

7. **Assign purpose to your money.** As you begin to see your savings account grow, it's easy to start imagining the many ways in which you can spend the money. This is where you must again exercise restraint and discipline. You can spend money and have it decrease and have no long-term benefit, or you can spend money and have it increase your value. Every decision to spend your money should be preceded by the question, "Does this increase my value?" Until you have achieved a stable financial foundation, every decision to spend money should be to increase, not decrease, your net worth. You do this by engaging in financial activities that bring value to your life, not the lives of others. Assigning purpose to your money will give you the opportunity to take control over your life and finances without feeling helpless.

A very important point to note is that the application of the "Power of No" exercise and establishing the "No Account" is based on use of a cash system. If you would normally use a credit card, you need to decide to only spend cash until you have a handle on your spending. Initially you will be saying no to the use of the credit card. In this case, have a section for credit-card use only. Every time you say no to yourself or someone else in a scenario where you would have used your credit card, document the amount of credit you would have used. Tally this amount up daily and weekly. Does your salary cover the total amount of credit you would have used in addition to your other expenses? Or did you overspend? The total amount of money you decided not to charge to your credit card gives you an idea of the rate and amount of unnecessary credit you are using. This use of credit is taking away your ability to do anything purposeful with your money. It is taking away your right to your time, relationships, pleasure, and eventually future happiness.

I have given you some very basic advice on how to take control of your finances without the clutter of how to get things done. Failure to deal with the matters of the heart when it comes to finances will lead to financial ruin every time. Why? Because who we are and what we determine in our hearts to be the focus of our lives is where we will invest our time, energy, and resources. A twisted, unstable foundation produces poor decisions regarding finances and creation of wealth.

After reading this book, you may say it doesn't apply to you. But I will challenge you to document your spending habits for thirty days. I guarantee you that it will become evident to you that the majority of your problem is not that you aren't earning enough money; you just don't spend it correctly. You will see the content of your character displayed numerically on paper or whatever device you choose to journal on. It is said that numbers don't lie, and they certainly won't in this case.

When I coach people on money, my assignment is not to tell you how to invest or spend your money. I am a precursor to a financial advisor. My ultimate goal is to get you to a point where you recognize how *your decisions are creating your financial future. Your decisions will create wealth and true prosperity.* By helping you reach this point of realization, I can guarantee that if you adhere to the principles for handling money, you can and will create the financial future you desire, because you will have the money to do it with. You will then be ready for a financial advisor. By just telling yourself and other people no when it comes to your money, you will discover that you have savings without working an extra hour a day. Your use of cash and credit cards will decrease, giving you the extra cash to pay off debts in advance and the ability to work with a financial advisor to build a financially stable future.

Clients who fail my coaching program do so because they are reluctant to abandon old, destructive behaviors and attitudes toward money. They lack desire, determination, and mostly discipline in correcting the affairs of their lives and finances. They end up right back where they started or worse than before.

With the information in this book, you now have the ability to make positive changes in your life. Your ability to focus your spending toward the purpose you have established for your life will produce balance and happiness. It will create a sense of power and control. Your life becomes more meaningful.

Working in health care, I've been present with many people in the last days of their lives; from the very rich to the poor. Those who felt they had achieved some level of purpose and enjoyment in life were more welcoming of the end of their journey. On the other hand, there were others who wished they had more time and finances to do the things they desired. These persons required a bit more reassurance and redirecting of their focus from the negative feeling of under accomplishment.

While death is inevitable, it is what we do with our lives that really matter. Strive to build a strong financial foundation through focused spending. This financial foundation is the avenue through which you will accomplish your life's purpose. It is the foundation that will allow you to correct mistakes, make a difference in the world, positively impact others and your environment, and make your voice heard. Most importantly, a strong financial foundation allows you to have what you need for the travel time through a life filled with purpose.

Get actively involved with your money and start Moving in 3-D (desire, determination, and discipline)! You may not feel comfortable speaking to people about this very vulnerable area of your life. It's not easy to allow people to know that you don't understand how to handle your finances or even deal with your heart issues. But, in privacy you can implement these steps until you build confidence. When you are ready, reach out to people who have a proven track record of being qualified to work with you. Work with them to help you achieve purpose in life through focused spending. I pray that you will be successful in every step of your journey!

# ABOUT THE AUTHOR

Shawn Saunders is an International Money Coach, Inspirational Speaker, and Entrepreneur. She specializes in identifying counterproductive mindsets that hinder financial freedom and teaches beliefs, customs, and behaviors to shift an individuals' paradigm for foundational wealth, prosperity, and purposeful living.

For the past twenty-three years, Saunders has worked in pharmaceutical research, real estate, and ministry. She earned a Bachelor's degree from Barry University and a Master's degree from Florida International University.

Saunders is President of Empower To Prosper International and The Deborah House Project, a non-profit organization that assists pregnant teens and young mothers.

With her numerous accomplishments, Saunders has been featured in Black Enterprise magazine and various programs. She's also an ordained minister and the author of The Covenant of Peace. The proud mother of two children, she currently lives outside the Metro-Atlanta area in Georgia, USA.

For coaching, speaking engagements, or more information visit: www.shawn-saunders.com.